Valerie Briginshaw

An introduction to

# BENESH
# MOVEMENT
# NOTATION

# An introduction to
# BENESH MOVEMENT NOTATION

Its general principles and its use
in physical education

## MARGUERITE CAUSLEY

MAX PARRISH • LONDON

MAX PARRISH AND CO LTD
2 PORTMAN STREET LONDON W1


FIRST PUBLISHED 1967

MADE AND PRINTED IN GREAT BRITAIN BY PURNELL AND SONS LTD
PAULTON, BRISTOL

# FOREWORD

This book is intended for those concerned with all aspects of physical education, movement analysis, modern and ethnic dance and remedial work, who feel the need for a movement notation which is as precise, simple, economic, fast, universal and objective as the alphabet.

Since the basic principles are the same in all movement fields, this book will also be of interest to those engaged in specialised fields such as work study and neurology, even though it does not show how the notation has been developed and applied in such fields.

*To Rudolf and Joan Benesh*

I am deeply indebted to Joan Benesh for all the time she has given me. She has spared nothing in helping me to see clearly not only the logical progression of the notation but also how to adapt and develop my ideas so that they fit its logical progression. Without her this book could not have been written. Her help and patience in assisting me to devise a notation syllabus for use in movement education and checking the written examples of notated movement was invaluable to me.

I am also extremely grateful to Rudolf Benesh, the inventor of the notation, for his advice and encouragement. He has taught me the meaning of the term 'academic respectability'. His intelligent understanding of all my problems, hopes and ideas has helped me more than I can say. I should also like to thank him for his superb drawings.

# CONTENTS

# ACKNOWLEDGEMENTS

I wish to thank the following:

Miss A. J. Bambra, Principal of Chelsea College of Physical Education, Eastbourne, for invaluable encouragement and for giving me the chance to test my ideas in practice.

Gordon F. Curl, for giving me the opportunity to teach notation within his research project.

Ann Whitley, Assistant Librarian of the Institute of Choreology, for preparing the notation examples.

Doreen Bonaker, for typing the manuscript.

# INTRODUCTION

At the present time many teachers are finding that it is of great value to children to have movement taught as an integral part of their school studies; this teaching can only bring out the child's movement capacities to the full if it is based on a detailed and scientific study of human movement.

With the development of the creative aspect of movement many new and exciting possibilities are being opened up, and teachers are just beginning to understand how wide is the range of movement skills that children are able to master. On the one hand children are still enjoying, more than ever, their team games and other recreational activities; on the other hand they are finding opened up to them whole new fields of enjoyment, creative fulfilment and movement understanding in modern educational dance and gymnastics.

In almost every other field of educational development we take for granted the use of a precise, simple and economic notation. It is normal to come to grips with languages, mathematics and music by using the generally accepted notations for these subjects. A notation aids and develops memory and assists the student to test, analyse and study in depth; these things are just as important in movement as in other fields of study — for the extent of a student's development depends on his ability to retain and manipulate movement patterns in relation to his own individual thoughts and experiences.

In the study of human movement we have in the past tended to use various devices in an attempt to record movement experiences. These records are unfortunately much too vague and ambiguous; when read some time later they give us only a very general idea of the movement situations and are quite inadequate for complex patterns.

The trouble is that the amount of information needed to give an accurate, detailed and unambiguous record, on two-dimensional paper, of movements and salient positions of each part of the body, in three dimensions of space and one of time, is greater by at least two orders of magnitude than that needed to record speech and music; in fact it was only in recent decades, with the development of ergonomics, cybernetics and operational research, that it became possible even to take the measure of the problem.

The design of a notation system for use in physical education, science and technology must be such as to facilitate not only the recording of all

9

forms of movement, but also to make possible creative work, research and analysis. The notation must be a recording tool which is completely objective, i.e. neutral to all theories. It must have a logical structure derived from the medium: in the same way that the alphabet is phonetic, i.e. derived from the nature of speech, and music notation is derived from the nature of music, movement notation must be 'choretic'. It must show movements as well as salient positions. It must be universal, covering all forms, styles and techniques of movement, and coping equally well with free and skilled movements. It must conform to the way we form a kinaesthetic image of our bodily positions and movements. It must also conform to natural movements of hand and eye, and be capable of easy integration with other notations. It must be cursive (i.e. easily written). It must be simple (so that it remains easily legible even when recording complex material); practical under the most difficult conditions; extremely accurate; economic and fast (demanding the minimum of paper and time); and complete (covering all parts of the body).

These last requirements seem contradictory. If a notation is to be complete and precise, it would seem to need a large number of symbols; on the other hand, if it is to be simple, practical, economic and fast, it must avoid any proliferation of symbols. The Benesh Movement Notation resolves this fundamental and apparently insoluble dilemma in a number of ways, at the same time coping with the other requirements set out above:

(a) It is completely visual, using marks on a matrix to record a great amount of information very simply, and coping with every imaginable position and movement with the same ease.

(b) It draws on centuries of development in music notation in recording changes through time.

(c) It uses movement lines which summarise an infinite number of records of salient positions.

(d) It cuts down redundancy to the minimum, giving only the information needed for a clear, precise and unambiguous record.

CHAPTER ONE

# FIRST CONSIDERATIONS

In writing down human movement one basic problem is to translate a three-dimensional position on to a two-dimensional surface. This is best done by using simple marks on a matrix which gives a clear visual analysis of the human body.

## A · The Stave

The five-line stave of music is ergonomically perfect and is the ideal matrix for the human figure. In addition it follows the natural pathway of eye and hand, left to right across the page.

Figure 1 shows how the lines of the stave intersect the body, when it is fitted in between the 5th line (top of the head) and the 1st line (the feet). The 4th line then cuts the body at the shoulder, the 3rd line at the waist and the 2nd line at the knees.

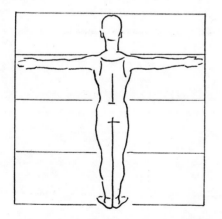

The line of the head.

The line of the shoulder.

The line of the waist.

The line of the knees.

The line of the feet.

Fig. 1

We look at the mover from behind. In this way the reader can positively identify himself with the movements written down. This way of recording salient positions corresponds to our kinaesthetic image.

The arm span equals the height of a body from head to feet, so that a person standing with his arms extended sideways conveniently occupies a square. This scale is used for all recording. For the beginner the stave can be divided into squares, to guide the eye, but this can soon be dispensed with.

## B · The Three Basic Signs

Imagine the person standing against a wall on which the five lines are marked. If you chalk a mark by the hands and feet the person is able to leave the 'wall' and a visual record of the body shape remains.

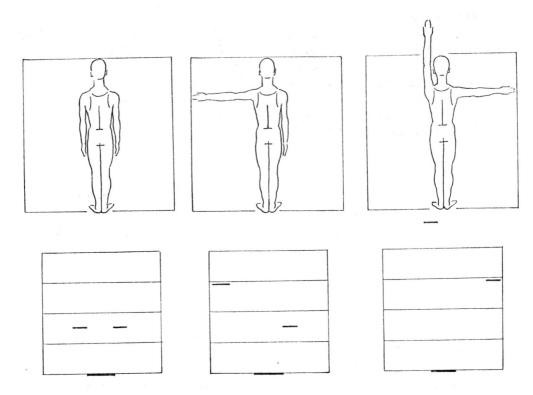

Fig. 2

The two-dimensional shape now needs to be developed into three-dimensional space, in which case the limb is either in front of the 'wall' or behind it.

The three basic signs are as follows:

—       LEVEL (with the body)

|       IN FRONT (of the body)

•       BEHIND (the body)

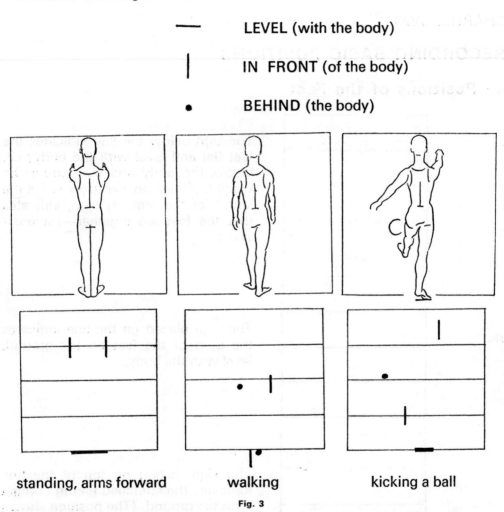

standing, arms forward      walking      kicking a ball

Fig. 3

No other information is needed. Since the limbs are of fixed length and are attached to the body at fixed points, the marking of the extremities gives a completely unambiguous record of positions with straight limbs.

# CHAPTER TWO

# RECORDING BASIC POSITIONS

## A · Positions of the Feet

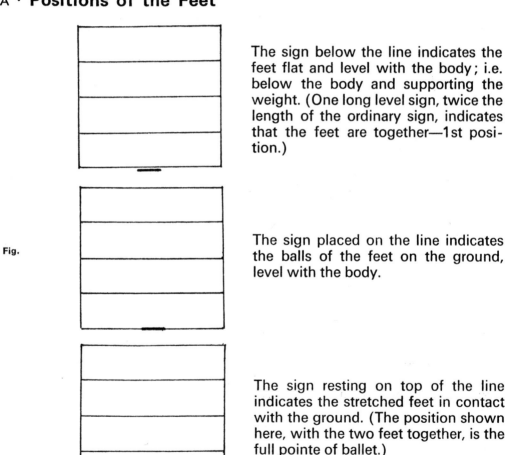

**Fig.**

The sign below the line indicates the feet flat and level with the body; i.e. below the body and supporting the weight. (One long level sign, twice the length of the ordinary sign, indicates that the feet are together—1st position.)

The sign placed on the line indicates the balls of the feet on the ground, level with the body.

The sign resting on top of the line indicates the stretched feet in contact with the ground. (The position shown here, with the two feet together, is the full pointe of ballet.)

## 1. Weight Evenly Distributed

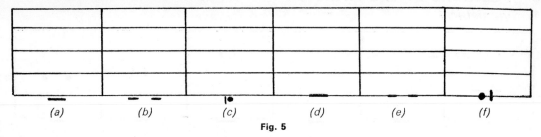

Fig. 5

(a)  1st position flat as above.

(b)  Two signs placed apart show the feet flat and astride. Any degree of width astride can be shown (2nd position).

(c)  The forward and backward signs illustrate standing with the left foot in front, right foot behind, weight evenly distributed (4th position).

(d)  1st position on balls of feet, as above.

(e)  2nd position on balls of feet.

(f)  4th position on balls of feet.

## 2. Weight on One Foot

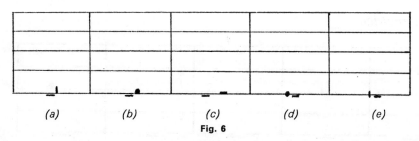

Fig. 6

(a)  Left foot level (i.e. under the body supporting the weight), right foot extended in front, tip of toe touching the ground.

(b)  Left foot level, right foot extended behind, tip of toe touching the ground.

(c)  Left foot level, right foot extended sideways, tip of toe touching the ground.

(d)  Right foot level, left foot extended backward, ball of foot touching the ground.

(e)  Right foot level, left foot extended forward, ball of foot touching the ground.

15

# B · Positions of the Arms

## 1. Symmetrical

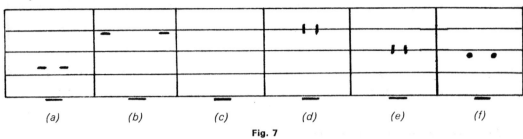

Fig. 7

(a) Normal position of the arms hanging by side of body. Note that the signs are separated by the width of the body.

(b) Arms extended sideways just below shoulder height.

(c) Arms extended directly above the head.

(d) Arms forward at shoulder height.

(e) Arms forward at waist height.

(f) Arms behind the body just below waist height.

## 2. Asymmetrical

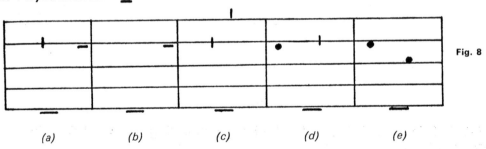

Fig. 8

(a) Left arm extended forward shoulder height, right arm extended sideways just below shoulder height.

(b) Left arm directly above the shoulder, right arm as in (a).

(c) Left arm forward at shoulder height, right arm extended forward and above the head.

(d) Left arm behind at shoulder height, right arm in front at shoulder height.

(e) Left arm to the side and behind just below shoulder height, right arm almost directly behind just above waist height.

16

## c · Combinations of Arm and Foot Positions

### 1. Symmetrical

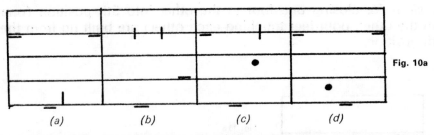

Fig. 9

(a) Feet together (1st position) arms by sides : normal standing position.

(b) Feet apart (2nd position), arms extended sideways, slightly below shoulder level.

(c) Feet apart (2nd position) on balls of feet, arms extended sideways just below top of head level – 'star' shape.

(d) Feet together (1st position) arms forward at shoulder height, slightly wider than normal shoulder width.

(e) Hands in front of thighs, feet together on balls of feet.

(f) Feet apart (2nd position) hands behind body extended out to the side above waist height.

### 2. Asymmetrical

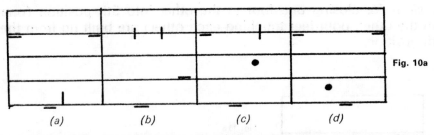

Fig. 10a

(a) Left foot level, right foot extended straight forward, tip of toe on the ground, arms extended sideways just below shoulder height.

(b) Arms extended forward at shoulder height, left leg extended sideways just above knee height.

(c) Right arm forward at shoulder height, left arm out to side, right leg extended behind at hip height.

(d) Both arms extended forward as in (b), left leg extended backwards and sideways just below knee height.

17

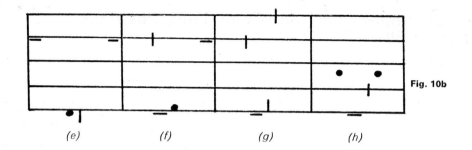

Fig. 10b

(e)    (f)    (g)    (h)

(e) Arms extended sideways at shoulder height, feet in 4th position (i.e. forward and backward, weight evenly distributed).

(f) Left arm extended forward at shoulder height, right arm sideways just below shoulder height, right foot extended backwards, tip of toe touching the ground.

(g) Right arm extended forward and upward above the head, left arm extended forward at shoulder height. Right foot forward, tip of toe touching the ground.

(h) Both arms extended behind just below waist level, right leg extended forward, foot at knee height.

## D · Closing the Feet

The signs for closing one foot to the other into 5th position (one foot behind the other, both feet touching each other) are built up from the sign for 5th position.

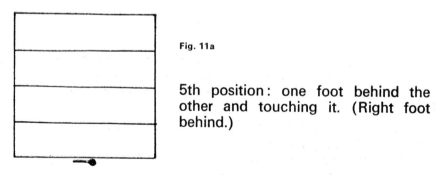

Fig. 11a

5th position: one foot behind the other and touching it. (Right foot behind.)

18

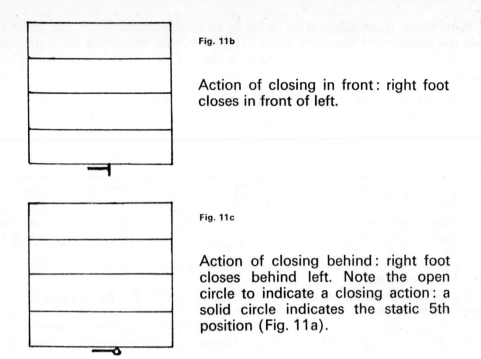

Fig. 11b

Action of closing in front: right foot closes in front of left.

Fig. 11c

Action of closing behind: right foot closes behind left. Note the open circle to indicate a closing action: a solid circle indicates the static 5th position (Fig. 11a).

## E · Bending the Limbs

The three basic signs used in sections B and C give a precise and complete record of the limbs when straight. To record the limbs bent in any position, three more signs are added: these mark the position of the knees and elbows on the stave. The sign for a bend is a cross.

The level sign is crossed with a short line to show the bent elbow or knee level with the body.

The front sign is crossed with a short line to show the bent elbow or knee in front of the body.

The dot of the back sign becomes an X to show the bent elbow or knee behind the body.

*19*

With these three signs it is possible to plot accurately on the stave the precise position of the bent limbs. Together with the signs for hands and feet they provide a complete visual picture of all possible positions of the limbs.

## F · **Positions of the Knees**
### 1. *Symmetrical*

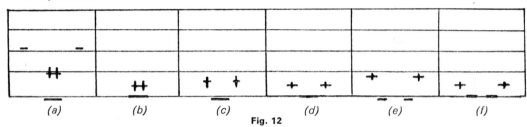

(a)  (b)  (c)  (d)  (e)  (f)

**Fig. 12**

(a)  Knees bent forward together, touching, just below their normal height, feet in 1st position.

(b)  A deep knee bend, knees touching. Note that the heels have risen, as normally happens.

(c)  1st position, knees apart, half bent and turned out to 45 degrees.

(d)  Knees deeply bent and fully turned out. Note that the heels have risen. Level cross indicates the outward rotation of the knees.

(e)  2nd position, knees slightly bent.

(f)  Similar to (e) with a deep knee bend and the feet slightly closer together, heels raised.

### 2. *Asymmetrical*

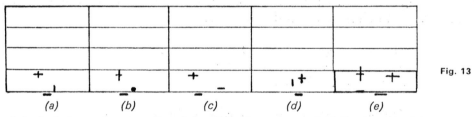

(a)  (b)  (c)  (d)  (e)

Fig. 13

(a)  Left knee bent to the side, right foot extended forward with tip of toe on the ground.

(b)  Left knee bent in front, weight on left foot, right foot extended behind, tip of toe on the ground.

(c)  Left knee bent to the side, the weight on the left foot, right leg extended sideways with foot lifted just above the ground.

20

(d) Right knee bent in front of the body, left leg extended forward, foot just below knee height.

(e) Left knee forward, left foot on the ball, right knee bent sideways, weight on the flat right foot.

## G · Positions of Elbows

### 1. Symmetrical

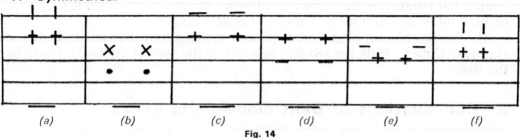

Fig. 14

(a) Elbows bent in front, shoulder height, with the hands directly above the elbows.

(b) Elbows forced back at chest height, hands immediately below them.

(c) Elbows bent to the side at shoulder height, hands immediately above them.

(d) Same as (c) except that the hands are immediately below the elbows.

(e) Arms make a W shape. Elbows are dropped level and into the side of body, just above waist height, hands angled out sideways just below shoulder level.

(f) Elbows bent forward at chest height, hands in front of face.

### 2. Asymmetrical

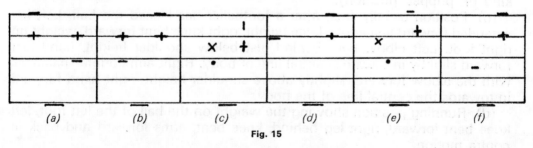

Fig. 15

(a) Elbows sideways at shoulder height, left hand immediately above left elbow, right hand immediately below right elbow.

(b) Opposite position to (a).

(c) Sprint action of the arms: left elbow behind at chest height, left hand behind at hip height, right elbow forward at chest height, right hand forward at face height.

(d) A policeman stopping traffic from both front and behind (Ref: P. 22 of Highway Code).

(e) Coalman carrying a sack. Left elbow behind just below shoulder height, left hand near body, behind at waist height. Right hand level above head, right elbow in front just above shoulder height.

(f) Policeman stopping a vehicle approaching from the front (P. 22 of Highway Code). Note the left arm straight by the side of the body. Hand by the thigh.

## H · Combinations of Bent Elbows and Knees

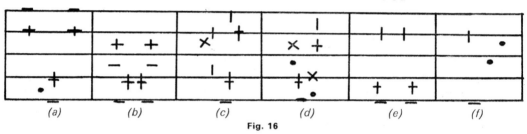

Fig. 16

(a) Elbows to the side, just below shoulder height, hands immediately above them. Right knee bent forward, weight on right foot, left leg is bent backwards between floor and knee height.

(b) Elbows bent to side, chest height, hands immediately below them. Knees bent forward, nearly touching, feet widely placed in 2nd position (a kind of 'puppet' position).

(c) Position usually seen after a footballer has kicked the ball. Left leg extended forward just above knee height, right knee bent forward, weight on right foot. Left elbow bent behind just below shoulder height, hand just forward slightly in towards central line of body. Right arm counter-balances with the elbow forward, slightly above shoulder height, right hand forward in towards the central line of the body.

(d) Running position showing the weight on the ball of the left foot, left knee bent forward, right leg behind, knee bent, arms forward and back in contra motion.

(e) Very wide spread at the legs, knees forward, arms extended forward at shoulder height. A position sometimes seen in Indian Dance.

(f) Return to position with limbs straight. Note that when limbs are straight, elbows and knees are not shown.

## I · Crossing Over the Central Line of the Body

When the foot or hand crosses over the central line of the body the sign is lightly crossed out with a diagonal stroke from right to left.

Hand or foot level with the body, crossed over the central line.

Hand or foot in front of the body, crossed over the central line

Hand or foot behind the body, crossed over the central line.

Elbow or knee in front of the body crossed over the central line.

There are no signs for the bent elbows and knees crossed behind, or level, because such positions are anatomically impossible.

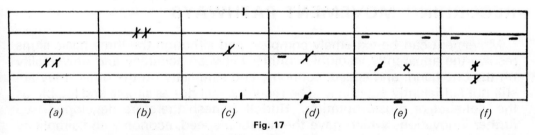

Fig. 17

(a) Hands crossed in front of thighs.

(b) Hands crossed, extended forward at shoulder height.

(c) Standing on left foot, tip of right foot touching ground diagonally forward, left hand crossed at waist height and extended forward. Right hand extended diagonally forward at head height.

(d) Weight on left foot, right foot crossed behind, resting on tip of toe. Right arm extended forward and crossed, left arm extended to the side, both just below waist height.

(e) Weight on left foot, right knee bent behind with foot crossed behind in line with knee as in ballet.

23

(f)  Right knee and foot crossed to left, weight on left foot. (As seen in national dance steps.)

This chapter has provided a brief introduction to the use of the basic signs. Together they make possible the precise recording of a very wide variety of positions.

The reader who has worked through the examples will now be able to visualise the body shape on the stave, filling in the trunk and the limbs between the signs. It is possible to record movement using only these signs, showing a series of salient positions. But the recording of complex movements in this way would demand the use of a very large number of intermediate positions, and in fact movement is shown not only by position signs but also by movement lines.

CHAPTER THREE

# RECORDING MOVEMENT PATHWAYS

Movement can be extremely complex, and although the three basic signs resolve the apparently insoluble conflict between accuracy and universality on the one hand, and speed, economy and simplicity on the other, they are still not sufficiently economic. The record is still not as simple and legible as the alphabet or music notation.  Rudolf Benesh therefore developed two further innovations which gave the notation speed, economy and simplicity without any sacrifice of accuracy and universality.  One is the use of movement lines; the other is a system of showing positions only when they change.  (I shall explain the latter on page 27.)

Movement is continuous, not discrete like music and speech (which are made up of a limited number of notes and phonemes respectively) and so needs a very large number of records of salient positions to cope with all its potential complexities.  Using a movement line, however, one can trace the path of movement between salient positions, thereby summarising an infinite number of intermediate positions.

Fig. 18 shows a movement of the right leg when raised to the side, finishing at hip height.

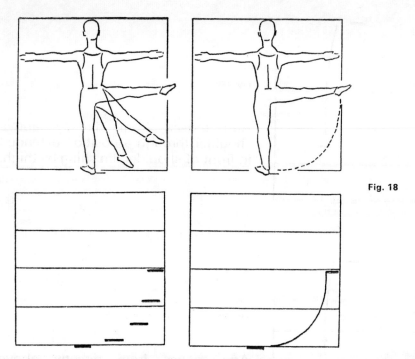

Fig. 18

Written like this, the movement lines show movement in the plane of the body. Arm movements are shown in the same way as leg movements.

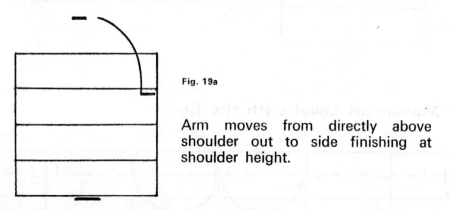

Fig. 19a

Arm moves from directly above shoulder out to side finishing at shoulder height.

If the line moves outside this plane this is indicated by a vertical dash or dot on the line, a logical development from the signs for salient positions in front of and behind the "wall".

25

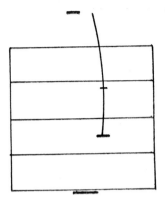

Arm moves from directly above shoulder through a position extended in front of shoulder, finishing by thigh.

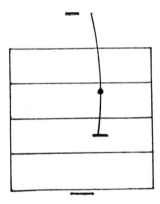

Fig. 19c

Arm moves from directly above shoulder through a position extended behind the shoulder, finishing by the thigh.

## A · Movement Level with the Body

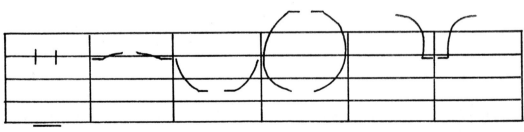

Fig. 20

*26*

This small study shows six arm positions and the movement pathways between them. The direction of movement is shown by attaching the basic sign at the end of the movement line, and omitting it at the beginning.

The study begins with the arms extended forward at shoulder height, close together. They open out to the side and then come down to the sides of the body. From here they make a wide sweeping curve until they are above the head; the right arm moves whilst the left remains in place and then the left arm moves. Both arms are now extended to the side. For purposes of speed and economy, only *changes* of positions are shown. Note that no foot positions are shown after the starting position, and in the last two frames only the moving arm is shown. This illustrates the fundamental principle of economy: throughout the notation positions are shown *when they change*, and if no position or movement line is shown it is to be understood that there is no change. (See also page 35.)

## B · Movement in Front of and Behind the Body

Fig. 21  An arm circling exercise

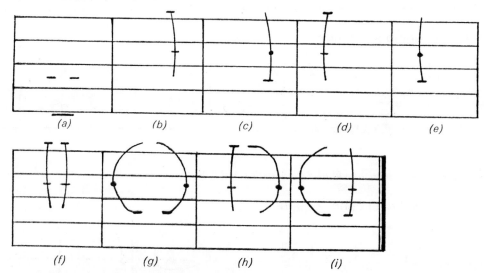

(a)         (b)         (c)         (d)         (e)

(f)         (g)         (h)         (i)

(a) Feet in 1st position, arms by side of body.

(b) Right arm makes a forward circling sweep to finish directly above the head.

(c) It returns to its previous position through a backward curved path.

(d) and (e) Left arm describes same pathway as in (b) and (c).

27

(f) Both arms move forward and upward simultaneously to arrive directly above the head.

(g) The arms made a wide backward sweeping curve, moving slightly behind to return to their original position (as in (a)).

(h) The left arm makes a forward curve and the right arm a broad backward curve, both to arrive directly above the head.

(i) Same as (h) but with opposite arms.

The above examples start and finish level with the body: the following examples start level and finish in front or behind.

An arm swinging sequence

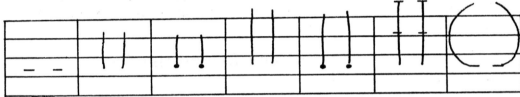

**Fig. 22**

A leg swinging sequence

**Fig. 23**

*The right leg swings forward and backward, higher and higher*

An arm and leg circling sequence

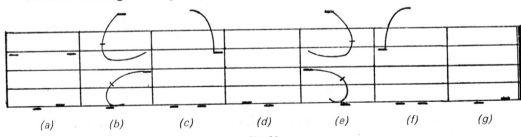

(a)　　　(b)　　　(c)　　　(d)　　　(e)　　　(f)　　　(g)

**Fig. 24**

(a) Arms extended to the side, right foot extended to the side, tip of toe touching the ground.

(b) A broad forward and sideways sweep of the right arm and leg.

(c) Right foot comes to the ground, right arm returns to original position with a sideways curve.

(d) A shift of weight shown, left foot extended to the side, tip of toe touching the ground.

(e), (f) and (g). A repeat of (b), (c) and (d) on left side of body.

## c · Movement Crossing Over the Central Line of the Body

Normally the movement line illustrates clearly that the limb crosses over the central line of the body and therefore there is no need to cross out the basic sign.

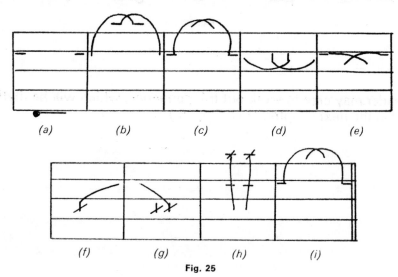

Fig. 25

Where the crossing over is not shown clearly (e.g. (f) or (g)), or where the movement lines are continued crossed (h), it is advisable to add the oblique crossing out for clarity.

## D · Combinations of Arm and Leg Movements

The movement lines can show very clearly simultaneous and consecutive movements of the arms and legs.

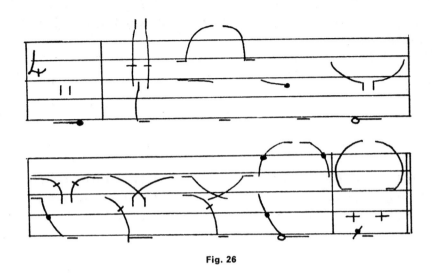

Fig. 26

The reader may care to work out this sequence, which will be rhythmically analysed in the next chapter. (See Fig. 28.)

# CHAPTER FOUR

# RHYTHM

Up to now we have been considering movements in isolation, but now we are ready to link them in rhythms and phrases; it is possible to dispense with the frames or squares since the eye can readily measure these off.

## A · Whole Beats

The stave is divided up into bars, as below. Note that in this example the beats are written above the stave and the bars are divided into beats by dotted lines: these are for guidance only, and are not part of the notation.

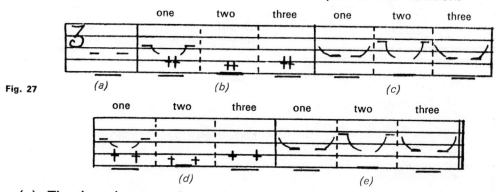

Fig. 27    (a)                (b)                (c)

(d)                (e)

(a)  The time signature shows three beats to a bar and the starting position of the body is given.

(b), (c), (d) and (e) Four bars each of three beats. There is a movement on every beat.

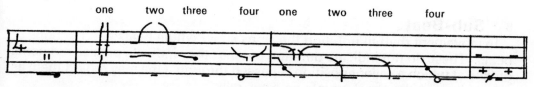

Fig. 28

The time signature shows that there are four beats to the bar. The eye measures off imaginary squares for each 'frame' of the movement. The finishing position is a curtsey.

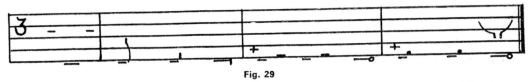

Fig. 29

The methods of showing rhythm characteristic of music notation are quite unsuited to movement notation. Movement is continuous, whereas notes are discrete sounds at a definite pitch, lasting a definite length of time, and sometimes separated from adjoining notes by rests of a definite length of time. The musical symbols used to indicate the duration of notes and rests have no meaning in movement, which needs its own rhythm notation.

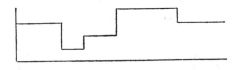

Music as a series of discrete sounds of definite pitch and duration.

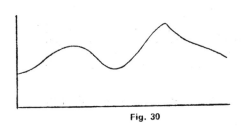

Movement as a continuity.

Fig. 30

## B · Sub-Beats

In movement rhythm notation the signs show whole beats and fractions of beats. These do not indicate duration of time : they indicate precise moments of time at which a salient position is passed through. One may regard them as something like the check points on a car-rally.

The rhythm notation is only used when the rhythm is irregular. Irregular rhythms are shown either by sub-beat signs or – when there is no basic sign indicating a salient position – by whole-beat signs. It is important to show

*32*

each beat in one way or another: i.e. either by a basic sign (on the stave) or by a whole-beat sign (above the stave).

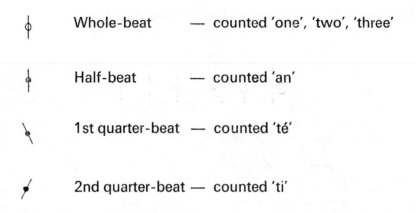

| | Whole-beat | — counted 'one', 'two', 'three' |
| | Half-beat | — counted 'an' |
| | 1st quarter-beat | — counted 'té' |
| | 2nd quarter-beat | — counted 'ti' |

## c · Rhythmic Patterns

1. Let us start with a polka rhythm counted as follows:

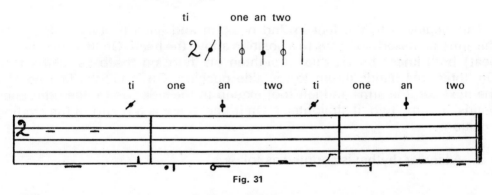

Fig. 31

The above example shows how movement in a definite rhythm is notated. Instead of starting on the first beat of the bar the phrase of movement in Fig. 31 starts on 'ti', the preceding weak beat (anacrusis); on this sub-beat the right foot is extended forward, then it is put down in fourth position on the beat at the beginning of the first bar. ('one'). Then on the 'an' the left foot is closed behind the right; here a half-beat is shown. On 'two' the right foot is extended to touch the floor at the side, on 'ti' the right foot is raised to the side just below knee height. On 'one', the first beat of the second bar, the right foot is closed in front of the left. On 'an' (half-beat marked as such), the right foot is extended to touch the floor at the side: on 'two' the weight is transferred to the right foot.

2. A mazurka rhythm is counted as follows:

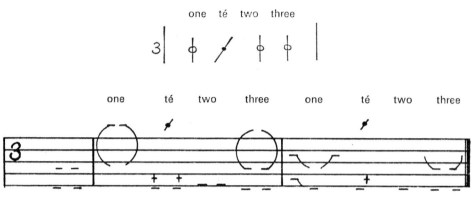

Fig. 32

This begins with the feet in 2nd position and arms by thighs. On 'one' the arms are raised sideways to a position above the head. On 'ti' (3rd quarter-beat) both knees bend; they straighten on 'two' on the balls of the feet. On 'three' the hands return to the side position. On 'one', the first beat of the next bar, the arms and left foot extend to the side. On 'ti' the right knee bends, and on 'two' it straightens. On 'three' there is a return to the starting position.

3. A ländler rhythm is counted as follows:

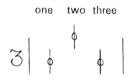

Note that the movement is held on the second beat, and that this is shown by writing the sign higher than the others.

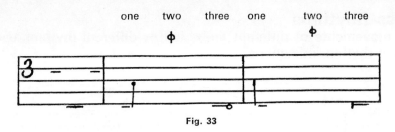

one    two    three    one    two    three

Fig. 33

Fig. 33 begins with feet together and arms extended to the side. On 'one' the right leg is raised behind and held in this position for 'two'. Because there is no movement written the whole-beat is shown at 'two'. On 'three' the right foot closes behind the left foot. On 'one' (first beat of second bar) the left foot is raised in front and held there for the next beat. On 'three' the left foot closes in front of the right.

Note that the hand positions are shown at the beginning of this phrase, but are not shown subsequently. This represents the application of the basic principle of economy, achieved through eliminating redundancy.

4. The complications of compound time (jig, etc.) are avoided by the simple expedient of using third-beats. For example, 6/8 is written as two beats with third-beats.

### D · Use of the Legato Phrase Mark

When a phrase of movement lasts more than one beat, this is shown by a legato phrase mark, as in music. The shape of the whole movement is shown in the final 'frame' which has both movement lines and basic signs indicating the final position. The *time* occupied by the movement is shown by the phrase mark, which begins where the movement begins and ends over the final 'frame'.

Adagio

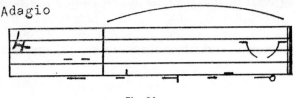

Fig. 34

The feet take up four different positions on each whole-beat: the arm movement shown at the end of the bar takes the whole bar, as indicated by the phrase mark.

*35*

## E · Cross-Rhythms

Where movements of different limbs follow different rhythms each limb has its own rhythm indications.

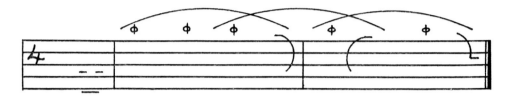

Fig. 35

The right arm starts on beat 'one' and moves over the four beats of the bar. The left arm starts halfway between the second and third beats and continues into the second bar, finishing on the second whole-beat. The right arm again moves over the four beats of the second bar, as in the first bar.

The same cross-rhythm can be written more simply and legibly as follows:

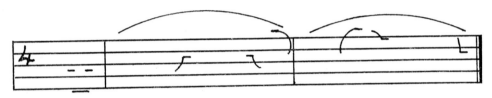

Fig. 36

In this case the relative position of the two arms is shown at different points, so that it is easy to interpolate between these points and to see how the arm movements are correlated.

The examples given in this chapter show dance rhythms: but rhythm is characteristic of all human movement, and in fact exactly the same method is used for recording rhythm in gymnastics, athletics, games, swimming, work study, remedial exercises and physiotherapy, neurology, etc.

CHAPTER FIVE

# LOCOMOTION ON THE FEET

It is now possible, by combining the basic signs and the movement lines, to show stepping, jumping, running, sliding, etc.

## A · **Stepping**
### 1. In Place

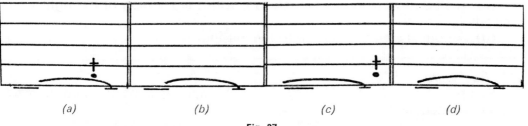

(a)          (b)          (c)          (d)

**Fig. 37**

(a) A step in place (i.e. on the spot, 'marking time'). A movement line is drawn from the right-hand side of the sign for 1st position, indicating that the *right* foot makes the stepping action. (If it were the left foot it would start from the left side of the 1st position sign.) The movement line ends in the middle of the basic sign for the right foot, indicating that the movement is in place. The fact that the right foot does the stepping is made doubly clear in bar 1 by showing the position of the left foot at the end of the step.

(b) Same as (a) written in simplified form because the left leg has not moved.

(c) As in (a) but the left foot performs the stepping action and the final position of the right foot is shown.

(d) As in (b) but on the left foot.

### 2. Forward
In order to show that the step is forward the front sign is added to the movement line.

37

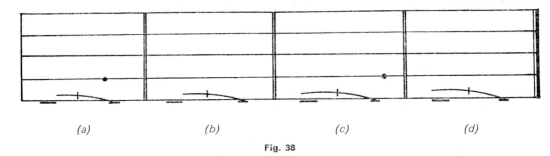

(a)          (b)          (c)          (d)

Fig. 38

(a)  A step forward on to the right foot with a clear indication of the final position of the left foot.

(b)  As in (a) but with the position of the left leg omitted.

(c)  A step forward on to the left foot with the position of the right foot clearly indicated.

(d)  A normal step forward on to the left foot.


### 3. Backward

Stepping backward is similarly shown by adding the backward sign to the movement line.

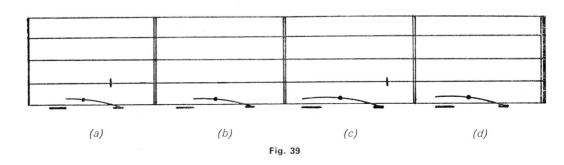

(a)          (b)          (c)          (d)

Fig. 39

(a)  A backward step on to the right foot whilst the left leg is extended forward at knee height.

(b)  A normal backward step on to the right foot.

(c)  (a) is shown on the other foot.

(d)  A normal backward step on to the left foot.

## 4. Combinations of Stepping Forward, Backward and In Place

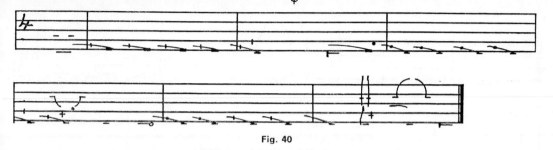

Fig. 40

The starting position is shown.

Bar 1. Four steps forward on to the *ball* of the foot, right, left, right, left.

Bar 2. Step forward on to right foot, left leg extended forward at knee height. Hold this position for one beat. The left foot joins the right foot in 1st position and then steps on to the ball, in place, right foot extended behind.

Bar 3. Four steps backward, right, left, right, left.

Bar 4. Step in place on right foot, left leg extended forward at knee height. Step forward on to left foot, bend the knee and extend the right foot behind, the arms opening out to the sides. Straighten the knee. Close the right foot into 5th position.

Bars 5 and 6. And so on.

## 5. To the Side.

To show a stepping action to the side, the movement line ends to the right or left of the basic level sign.

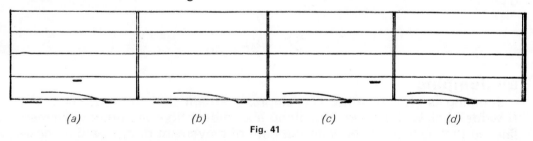

(a)    (b)    (c)    (d)

Fig. 41

(a) A step to the right, position of left foot indicated.
(b) A normal step to the right.
(c) A step to the left, position of right foot indicated.
(d) A normal step to the left.

## 6. Stepping in Rhythm

Fig. 42

Eight bars of stepping in waltz time. The legato phrase mark (bars 1 and 3) shows the arms moving continuously over a series of steps. Bars 2 and 4 show held positions of the arms after a step on the first beat of the bar.

## 7. Stepping in General

In a step the foot that initiates the movement takes the weight. When a series of steps is notated it is obvious which foot does the stepping because these must alternate. The first step is always clearly shown as right or left and the rest can be read in sequence.

Diagonal steps are written by combining the front or back sign and the sideways stepping movement line in such a way as to indicate the precise direction.

## B · Jumping

Jumping is shown rather like stepping except that the movement line is written below the stave. The 'jump line' differs from the other movement lines in that instead of showing the path of movement of one limb it shows the movement of the whole body.

## 1. Jumping in Place
### (i) Symmetrical

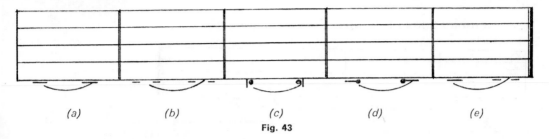

Fig. 43

(a)  A jump from two feet to two feet (1st position).

(b)  A jump from two feet to two feet (2nd position). When there is a landing with the feet apart (2nd and 4th positions) the movement line is drawn to finish between the two signs and to touch the bottom line of the stave.

(c)  A jump from two feet to two feet in 4th position with a change to the opposite 4th position.

(d)  A jump from two feet to two feet with a change to the opposite 5th position.

(e)  A jump from 1st to 2nd position.

### (ii) Asymmetrical

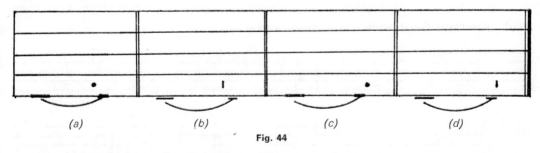

Fig. 44

(a)  A jump from both feet on to the ball of the right foot, the left leg extending behind.

(b)  A jump from two feet on to the flat of the right foot, left leg extending in front.

(c)  A jump from two feet on to the ball of the left foot, right leg extending behind.

41

(d)  A jump from two feet on to the flat of the left foot, right leg extending in front.

(iii)  Combinations of Jumps : Five basic jumps

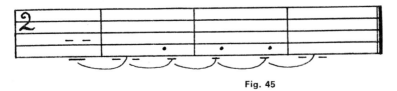

Fig. 45

Two to two, two to one, one to the other, one to the same, one to two.

(iv)  Body Shape During the Jump

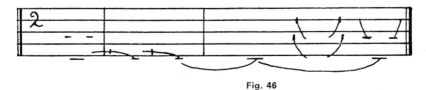

Fig. 46

In bar 2 the movement lines and the basic signs for hands and feet show the body shape in the air during the jump.

(v)  Jumping Sequence on a Trampoline

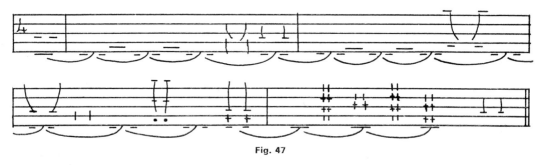

Fig. 47

The normal open position of the feet during the bounce on the bed and the closing of the feet in the air are shown. In the jumps where a definite shape is made, the precise position taken up can be written. The abrupt stop by flexing the knees, characteristic of trampoline work, is also shown at the end of the sequence.

## 2. Travelling Jumps
The direction of these is shown by modifications of the basic jump line.

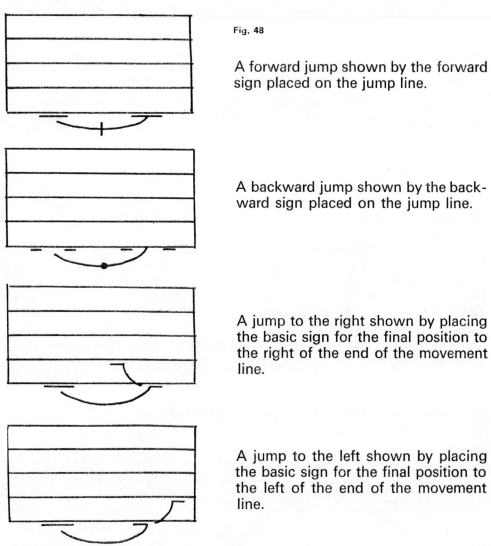

Fig. 48

A forward jump shown by the forward sign placed on the jump line.

A backward jump shown by the backward sign placed on the jump line.

A jump to the right shown by placing the basic sign for the final position to the right of the end of the movement line.

A jump to the left shown by placing the basic sign for the final position to the left of the end of the movement line.

43

## A sequence of travelling jumps

Allegro

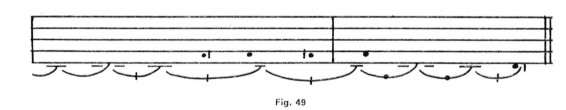

Fig. 49

Bar 1. Jump forward in 2nd position. Jump forward on to right foot, left leg extending behind. Jump in place into 5th position and jump in place into opposite 5th position.

Bar 2. Two jumps backward in 2nd position, jump to right extending left leg to the side, jump to left extending right leg to side.

Bar 3. Jump in place into 1st position, jump in place into 2nd position, jump forward into 1st position, jump forward on to right foot. (Note that the position of the feet during the jump is shown.) Repeat this jump landing on the left foot on the first beat of bar 4.

Bar 4. Jump backward into 2nd position, jump backward into 1st position, jump forward into 4th position.

## 3. Combination of Jumps and Arm Movements

Allegro

Fig. 50

On the second beat of bar 3 the arms move whilst the legs remain in the previous position. Elsewhere the arm movements exactly match the jumps.

## 4. Hopping

A hop is a jump from one foot to the same foot.

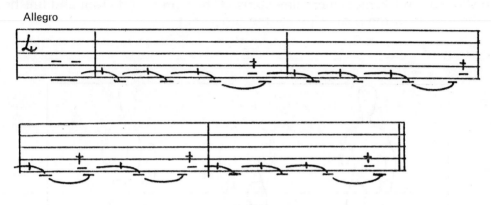

Fig. 51

Bars 1, 2 and 4 show three steps followed by a hop. Bar 3 shows step hop, step hop. In each hop the position of the non-hopping leg is shown and this, in conjunction with the previous step, indicates clearly that it is a hop.

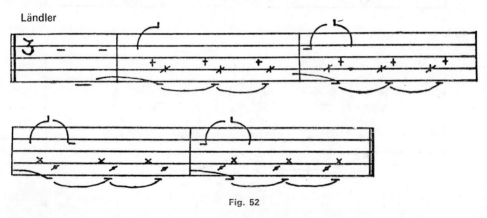

Fig. 52

Part of a Ländler dance, showing a step hop hop, phrase on alternate feet with corresponding arm movements. Note that the arms and free leg are

45

placed in position on the first beat of the bar and remain in the same position for the rest of the bar. Note also the crossed positions of the free foot in front of or behind the hopping leg.

## c · Running

The action of running is a series of jumps from one foot to the other foot. To show a run the movement line starts at the sign for one foot and finishes in the middle of the basic sign for the other foot.

### 1. Forward

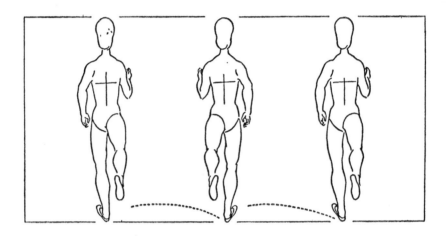

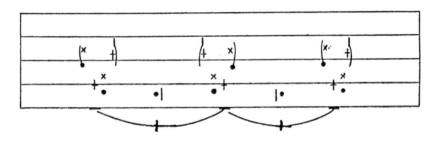

Fig. 53

In order to make clear the principles of the notation for running, the above example shows running analysed in great detail. (Any movement can be

46

written in a finely analysed way or in a way which is clear and unambiguous but does not show all the small details).

Fig. 54

The same run notated in the usual condensed manner. A run forward on to the left foot and then on to the right foot. At the beginning of the phrase the right leg is shown taking the weight and it is clear that the first run is on to the left foot (see Fig. 76, page 65).

## 2. In Place and Backward

In place and backward running is shown using the same logic as in the corresponding aspects of jumping. A plain jump line finishing in the centre of the level sign indicates a run in place; a dot on the jump line indicates a backward run.

## 3. Running in Rhythm

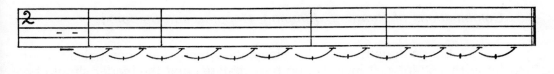

Fig. 55

Bars 1 and 3 show two running steps to the bar. (One on each beat.)

Bars 2 and 4 show forward runs on every half-beat. Because no rhythm notation signs are used it is evident that the runs are evenly spaced within each bar.

47

## 4. Running in Irregular Rhythms

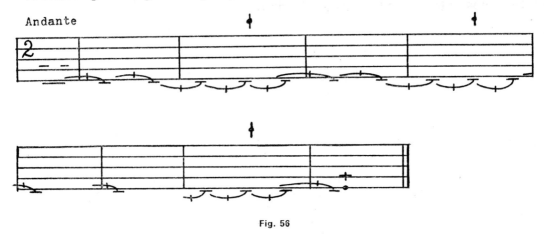

Andante

Fig. 56

Bars 1 and 3 show steps on each beat.

Bars 5, 6 and 8 show a step on the first beat, which is held for the rest of the bar.

Bars 2, 3 and 7 show three forward runs. The rhythm notation sign indicates the first beat divided into 'one an', the whole bar being counted 'one an two'.


## 5. Combinations of Running, Jumping, Hopping and Stepping

Fig. 57 brings together all the elements which have been dealt with so far in this chapter. It includes no new material and the reader should be able to follow without difficulty the notation on the page opposite.

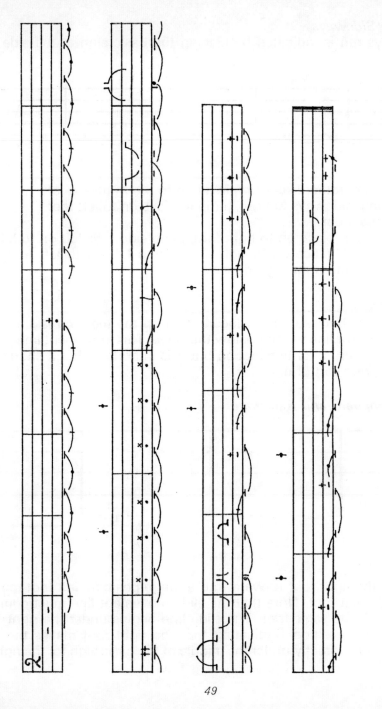

Fig. 57

## 6. Running Sideways

A sideways run is indicated by placing the basic sign at the side of the jump line.

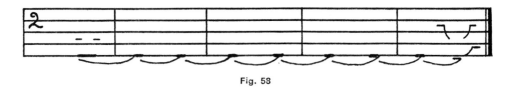

Fig. 58

These runs are rather like a simple galop to the right and left.

Bar 1. Jump sideways to right, jump in place on to left foot.

Bar 2. Repeat bar 1.

Bar 3. Jump in place on to right foot, jump sideways left on to left foot.

Bar 4. Jump in place on to right foot, jump left on to left foot, whilst extending arms and right leg sideways.

## D · Sliding

Sliding is the third method of locomotion on the feet and is shown by a straight movement line written below the stave. This movement line does not join the basic sign at its termination but it is important that it should finish under the correct part of it.

### 1. Sliding Forward and Backward

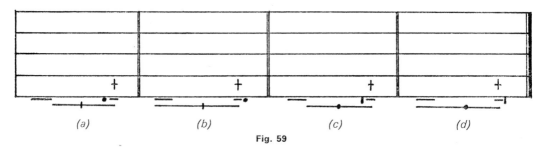

(a)          (b)          (c)          (d)

Fig. 59

(a) Slide the right foot forward into a lunge position, left foot remaining behind on the flat foot. Note that the slide movement line must commence and finish with the same foot. The slide line begins under the right side of the sign for 1st position (indicating that the right foot makes the sliding action) and ends directly under the middle of the basic sign for the right foot.

(b)  Same as (a) but sliding the left foot. (Note slide line from left side of sign for 1st position.)

(c)  Sliding the right foot backward into a lunge.

(d)  Sliding the left foot backward into a lunge. (Note in (c) and (d) that the front foot is left forward on the flat of the foot.)

## 2. Sliding to the Side

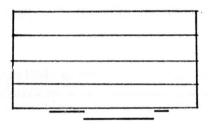

Slide the right foot to the right. Note that the basic sign for the finishing position is placed to the right, immediately above the end of the slide line : this indicates a slide to the right.

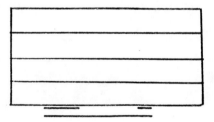

Slide the left foot to the left. Note that that the basic sign for the finishing position is placed to the left immediately above the end of the slide line : this indicates a slide to the left.

Fig. 60

## 3. *Slides of the Feet, Right and Left, with Hops and Jumps*

Tempo di Mazurka

Fig. 61

Bar 1. Slide right foot to the right, hop in place on right foot, jump in place into 1st position.

Bar 2. Repeat to the other side.

There is no space to give all the variations of locomotion on the feet in this short introduction. Steps such as crossing over, diagonal stepping, swishing and brushing the feet, low bounces and small hops are all simply and fully covered by the notation.

CHAPTER SIX

# DIRECTION SIGNS

We have already dealt with travelling forward, backward, sideways and so on in relation to the individual.

It is also necessary to show the direction faced in relation to the working area.

## A · Static Positions

A dancer may face the audience, a carpenter his bench, the athlete the throwing area, the gymnast his apparatus; in all cases a front needs to be established in relation to the working area.

The direction sign is an arrow in which the point has been reduced to a dot. This is written below the stave underneath the movement it refers to.

Facing front

Other directions are shown by changing the position of the sign.

Facing right

Fig. 62a                Facing left

Facing back

Facing right front diagonal

Facing left back diagonal

Any other direction of facing can be precisely shown

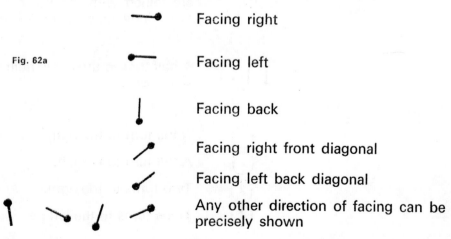

53

Applying the basic principle of economy, we do not normally show a direction sign at the start of the movement sequence if the mover is facing front. When we do show a sign indicating a direction of facing, the mover is to be understood as continuing to face in that direction until another direction sign is given.

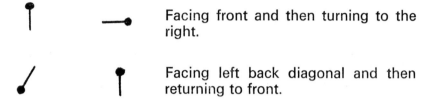

Facing front and then turning to the right.

Facing left back diagonal and then returning to front.

Fig. 62b

## B · Turning

Turning, whether on the ground or in the air is basically only a change of front. The direction sign is adapted to show the movement through a series of directions.

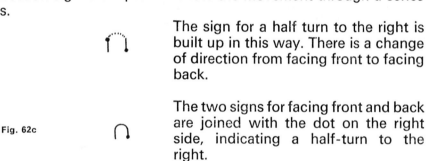

The sign for a half turn to the right is built up in this way. There is a change of direction from facing front to facing back.

Fig. 62c

The two signs for facing front and back are joined with the dot on the right side, indicating a half-turn to the right.

A half turn to the left is built up in the same way.

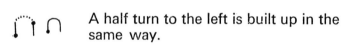

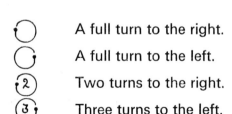

A full turn to the right.

A full turn to the left.

Two turns to the right.

Three turns to the left.

54

Other turns can be shown by building up from the basic signs in the same way.

**Fig. 62d**

One and a quarter turns right.

One and an eighth turns left.

One and a half turns right.

One and a half turns left.

Note that the beginning of the turning sign and the dot at the end indicate the starting and stopping positions. Because these turning signs are built up from direction signs they can show turns starting from any direction and ending in any direction.

## C · Sequences Showing Directions Faced and Turns

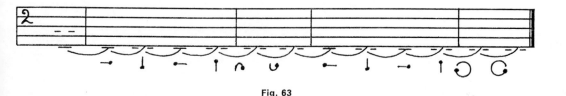

Fig. 63

N.B. In the descriptions given below, right, left, front etc. refer to the working area.

Start in 1st position facing front.

Bar 1. Turning jump in 1st position to face right; turning jump into 2nd position to face back; turning jump into 1st position to face left; turning jump into 2nd position to face front. Note that the jumps are in a rhythm which is counted, 'one an two an'.

Bar 2. Turning jump in to the right in 2nd position to face back; turning jump to the right in 2nd position to face front.

Bar 3. Same as bar 1 but in the opposite direction.

Bar 4. A complete jumping turn to the right in 2nd position; repeat to the left.

The following sequence shows a phrase from a national dance with hopping, running and stepping, and signs for directions faced and turns. No new signs are included and the reader should be able to follow the sequence quite easily.

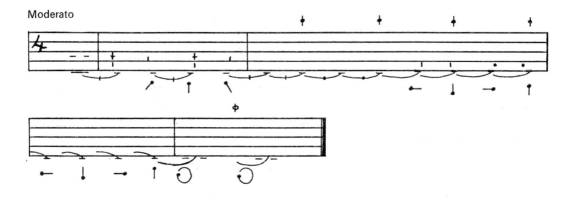

Fig. 64

# CHAPTER SEVEN

# MOVEMENTS OF THE HEAD AND TRUNK

## A · The Head

As Fig. 1 showed on p. 11, the head falls between the 5th and 4th lines.

A short vertical line which touches both lines and fills the whole space indicates the head in its normal position. If the head is bent forward or backward this is shown by a small horizontal line across the basic sign.

This may be regarded as representing the position of the chin. (Note that a bend is shown by a cross: this is consistent with other signs for bends.)

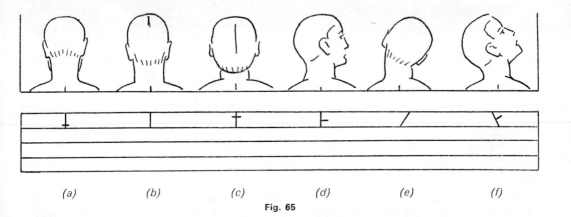

(a)                (b)                (c)                (d)                (e)                (f)

**Fig. 65**

(a)  A short line drawn across the basic sign for the head below the centre of the space indicates that the head bends forward.

(b)  Normal — Not usually written unless head returns to normal position after having performed a previous movement. (Note that the sign occupies the whole space between the lines.)

(c)  The head bends backward.

(d)  The head turns to the right.

(e)  The head tilts to the right.

(f)  A combination of (d) and (e).  The head turns and tilts.

All combinations of tilts, turns and bends in the head can be shown by using combinations of the above signs.

## B · The Trunk

Bends, turns and tilts of the trunk are shown in much the same way as those of the head. The signs for the trunk occupy the spaces between the 2nd and 4th lines. These two spaces show the two main divisions of the trunk: above the waist and below the waist.

As with the sign for the head, the signs for the trunk occupy the whole space between the lines.

## 1. The Waist

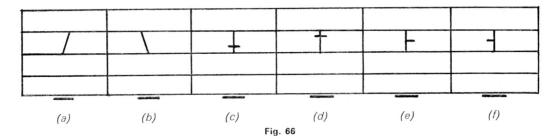

(a)       (b)       (c)       (d)       (e)       (f)

Fig. 66

(a) A tilt sideways to the right from the waist. Note that the spine and head move as one unit: if the head moved away from a position in line with the spine, this would be shown using the top space of the stave.

(b) A tilt sideways to the left from the waist up.

(c) A bend forward from the waist. Note that the crossed line is used to indicate the bend in exactly the same way as a bend of the head.

(d) A bend backward from the waist up.

(e) A twist to the right from the waist up.

(f) A twist to the left from the waist up.

## 2. The Hips

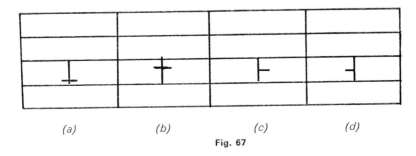

(a)       (b)       (c)       (d)

Fig. 67

(a) A bend forward from the hips.

(b) A bend backward from the hips.

(c) A twist to the right from the hips.

(d) A twist to the left from the hips.

58

# c · Combinations of Head and Trunk Movements

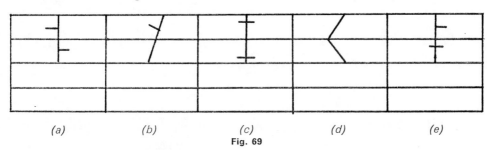

(a)          (b)          (c)          (d)          (e)          (f)

**Fig. 68**

(a) A bend forward from the waist up; head also bends forward.
(b) A bend backward from the waist up; head also bends back.
(c) A tilt to the right from the waist up; including the head.
(d) A tilt to the left as in (c).
(e) A right turn of the head, combined with a twist to the right of the trunk from the waist up.
(f) As in (e) but to left.

# D · Contrary Body Movements

Combinations of signs can be used to show contrary body movements.

(a)          (b)          (c)          (d)          (e)

**Fig. 69**

(a) A twist to the right from the waist up combined with a left turn of the head. Note that the head appears to remain static.
(b) A tilt to the right of the trunk from the waist up, the head moving with the trunk, combined with a left turn of the head.
(c) A bend forward from the waist combined with a bend backward of the head.
(d) A tilt of the trunk to the left combined with a right tilt of the head.
(e) A bend backward from the waist up combined with a right turn of the head.

## E · **Combinations of Twisting and Turning**

The methods of showing on the one hand turns of the whole body, and on the other hand twists of the trunk and turns of the head, are quite different, and no confusion is possible between these.

Allegro

Fig. 70

In these turning jumps there is a turn of the head in the opposite direction to that of the whole body, and a twist from the waist up in the same direction. Note that twists and turns of parts of the body are plotted on the stave, while those of the body as a whole are shown below the stave.

## CHAPTER EIGHT

# DYNAMICS

By adapting the expression marks etc. of music we can record the finest shades of effort, changes in effort, and other qualities of movement.

The technical words and expression marks of music have been developed over centuries of practical use and are equally applicable to all kinds of movement; dance, games, remedial work, work study etc.

## A · Degrees of Effort

Degrees of loudness in music are indicated by f (forte), ff, p (piano), pp etc. and the same letters are used in movement to indicate degrees of effort. (Here effort is used in its normal meaning as distinct from the broader meaning in which it is used in Laban Art of Movement.)

There is a scale of seven degrees of effort:

| | |
|---|---|
| ppp | completely relaxed |
| pp | very soft |
| p | soft |
| (no sign) | normal |
| f | strong |
| ff | very strong |
| fff | maximum strength |

## B · Changes of Effort

Changes of effort can be shown in much the same way as in music with diverging lines indicating increasing effort and converging lines indicating decreasing effort. Letters at the beginnings and ends of the lines show degrees of effort at these points: the principle is the same as that of the combination of basic signs for salient positions with movement lines.

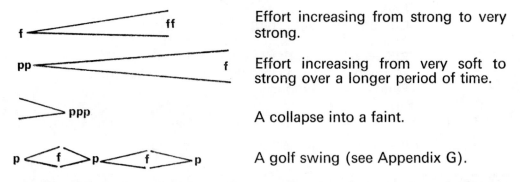

Effort increasing from strong to very strong.

Effort increasing from very soft to strong over a longer period of time.

A collapse into a faint.

A golf swing (see Appendix G).

For physical educationists who are used to the classification of Laban's eight efforts, the study given in Fig. 71 shows how effort-actions are notated. In Laban terminology 'effort' has three elements: spatial (pathway), temporal (speed) and strength. The movement line indicates the pathway, the musical term or metronomic indication indicates speed and the letters for p etc. indicate the strength.

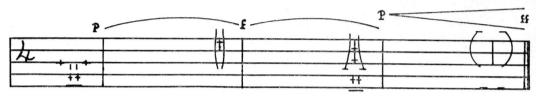

Fig. 71

Bar 1. A glide – arms move softly upwards through a direct pathway.
Bar 2. A press – arms move strongly downwards through a direct pathway.
Bar 3. Shading between a glide and a press.

Sf (sforzando) is used with much the same significance as in music. It indicates a movement with the quality of a punch or kick. Sfff shows a very powerful thrust or punch.

## c · Qualities of Movement

The technical Italian words used in music notation to indicate the character, mood and speed of the music are used in exactly the same way to describe movement. For example:

| | |
|---|---|
| Largo | broad, slow, gliding, floating etc. |
| Lento | slow |
| Moderato | at a moderate pace |
| Presto | very fast |
| Con brio | with spirit |
| Agitato | quick, flicking, agitated |
| Staccato | sharp, stabbing |
| Marcato | with strongly emphasised accents |
| Furioso | furiously |

A few examples of different qualities of movement are given below.

Thrusting or machine-like movements (e.g. toy soldiers).

Marcato

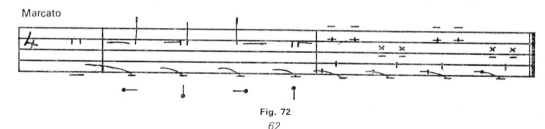

Fig. 72

## Strong swinging movements (slashing).

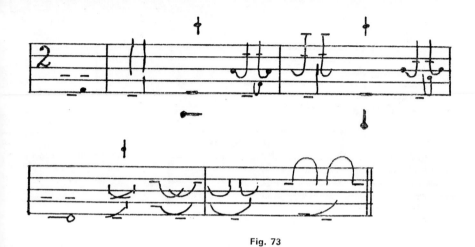

Fig. 73

## Smooth stepping with direct arm patterns (gliding).

Fig. 74

## A gymnastic sequence

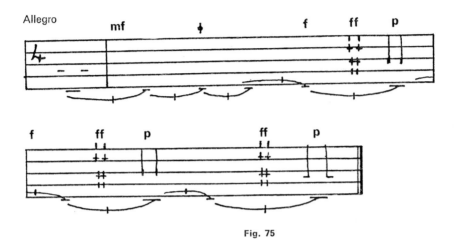

Fig. 75

Three runs, a step, and a very strong tuck jump (limbs bent forward close to the body). Land softly and then repeat the step – jump – landing sequence twice more.

# CHAPTER NINE

# KNEELING, SITTING AND LYING

These three actions have in common contact with the ground or a supporting object.

*The Contact Sign*

Contact is shown by a diagonal sign which is derived from the sign for the tilted first position. When the sign leans to the left it refers to the left foot or hand, when it leans to the right it refers to the right foot or hand.

The sequence given below shows the logic of the development of the contact from the sign for first position with the heel raised.

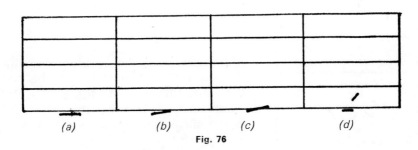

(a)       (b)       (c)       (d)

Fig. 76

(a)  1st position, both heels flat.
(b)  As (a) but the right foot has the heel raised.
(c)  Right foot raised so that the tip of the toe is in contact with the ground.
(d)  The right foot is raised in the air, and is now in contact with the side of the left leg.

Note that the knee is not shown since it must bend to enable the foot to take up this position. Of course any specific position of the knee can be shown if required.

c

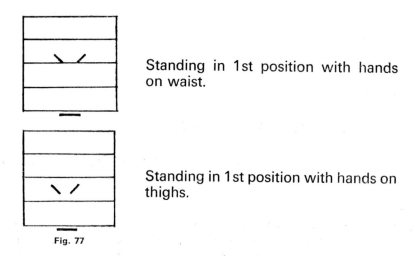

Standing in 1st position with hands on waist.

Standing in 1st position with hands on thighs.

Fig. 77

## Contact With Ground

When the contact is with the ground or other supporting surface or object the diagonal sign takes the form of a curved line which points downwards.

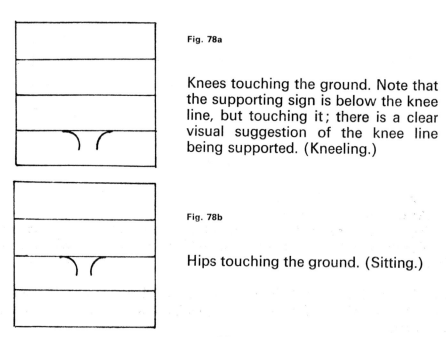

Fig. 78a

Knees touching the ground. Note that the supporting sign is below the knee line, but touching it; there is a clear visual suggestion of the knee line being supported. (Kneeling.)

Fig. 78b

Hips touching the ground. (Sitting.)

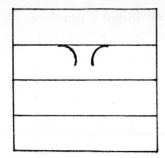

Fig. 78c

Shoulders touching the ground.

## A · Kneeling

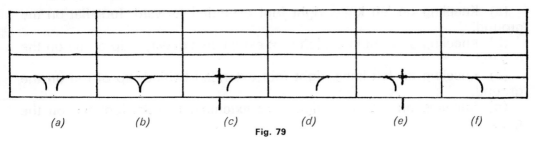

(a)　　　　(b)　　　　(c)　　　(d)　　　(e)　　　(f)

Fig. 79

    (a)  Kneeling, knees apart.
    (b)  Kneeling, knees together.
    (c)  Kneeling on right knee, left knee bent forward, left foot forward flat on the ground immediately below the knee (see below).
    (d)  Short version of (c) when position of left leg unimportant.
    (e)  Same as (c) but to the other side (see below).
    (f)  Short version of (e).

The reader may well wonder why in (c) and (e) a foot which lies directly below the knee is shown by a forward sign. This is done because whenever a body-bend is notated the stave is to be regarded as glued to the body and moving with it, so that there is no need to notate any movements of the body carried along with the bend. In kneeling positions on one knee the stave is to be regarded as glued around the bend of the knee in contact with the ground. In (c), for example, the stave follows the bend of the right knee; the left knee and foot are in front of the right knee and foot, and so are shown by forward signs.

Other positions of the non-kneeling leg can be shown if required.

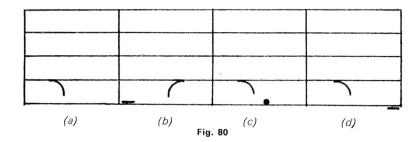

(a)       (b)       (c)       (d)

**Fig. 80**

   (a) Kneeling on left knee, right foot extended forward, foot flat on the ground.

   (b) Kneeling on right knee, left foot extended sideways, tip of toe on the ground.

   (c) Kneeling on left knee, right foot extended behind, tip of toe on the ground.

   (d) Kneeling on left knee, right foot extended to side, foot flat on the ground.


Rising from both knees.

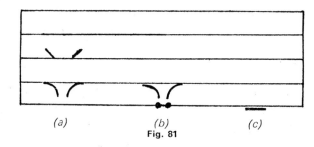

(a)       (b)       (c)

**Fig. 81**

   (a) Normal kneeling position, toes flat on ground behind body. Hands on waist.

   (b) Tuck feet under, so that the balls of feet touch the ground.

   (c) Stand up into 1st position.

68

Standing to kneeling.

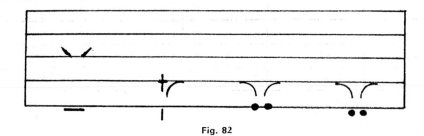

Fig. 82

From 1st position, standing up, drop on to right knee, then both knees, then stretch feet behind (i.e. take the balls of the feet off the ground).

Moderato

Fig. 83

Start in kneeling position.

Bar 1 : beat one. Right knee bends forward, right foot takes up a position immediately below the knee, weight remains on left knee which is still in contact with the ground, arms move forward to finish in front of shoulders.

Beat two. Right leg moves to the side finishing with tip of toe touching the ground, arms open to the sides.

Beat three. On the first half-beat a quick lifting action of the right leg. On the second half-beat the right leg returns to previous position.

Bar 2 : beat one. Right knee bends to the side, right foot flat on the ground immediately below the knee.

Beat two. Stand on right foot with right knee bent, left foot behind with tip of toe on the ground, arms move to a position in front of the head.

Beat three. Left foot closes behind right, arms lower through a forward pathway to finish in front of thighs.

69

## B · Sitting

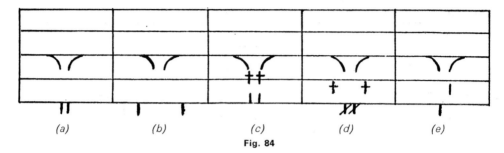

*(a)*            *(b)*            *(c)*            *(d)*            *(e)*

**Fig. 84**

(a)  Sitting with legs extended straight forward on the ground.
(b)  Sitting with legs astride.
(c)  Sitting with knees bent, tips of toes touching the ground.
(d)  Sitting cross-legged.
(e)  Sitting, left leg straight forward touching ground, right foot raised off
the ground.

Positions of the hands and feet whilst sitting.

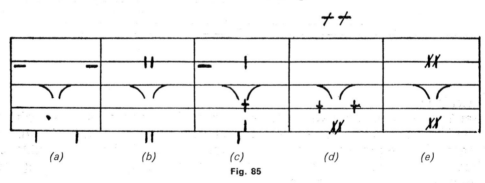

*(a)*            *(b)*            *(c)*            *(d)*            *(e)*

**Fig. 85**

(a)  Sitting, legs astride, arms extended to the sides.
(b)  Sitting, arms and legs straight forward.
(c)  Sitting, right knee bent, toe of right foot on the ground, right arm
forward, left leg straight on ground, left arm out to side.
(d)  Sitting, cross-legged, with tips of toes on the ground, hands crossed
above the head.
(e)  Sitting, legs extended forward and lifted off the ground with feet
crossed, arms extended forward crossed over.

70

## c · Lying

Lying is shown by using contact signs for shoulders and hips. It is assumed that the head is in contact with the floor: if it were lifted, a forward bend would be indicated on that part of the stave.

### 1. Supine (lying on the back)

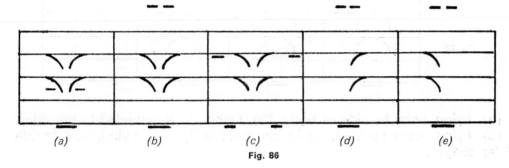

**Fig. 86**

(a) Lying, arms by side of body.
(b) Lying, arms above head, in line with the body.
(c) Lying, feet apart, arms extended to the side ('star' shape).
(d) Lying on right side.
(e) Lying on left side.

Supine lying with legs in more complex positions.

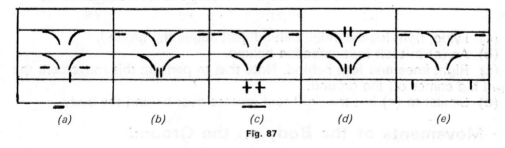

**Fig. 87**

(a) Lying, right leg raised forward.
(b) Lying, both feet raised forward.
(c) Lying, knees bent and slightly apart, feet on the ground.
(d) Lying, arms and feet raised forward.
(e) Lying, legs forward and astride.

71

## 2. *Prone* (lying on the front)

Prone lying is shown by reversing the supine lying signs, reflecting the fact that the body has rotated through 180°.

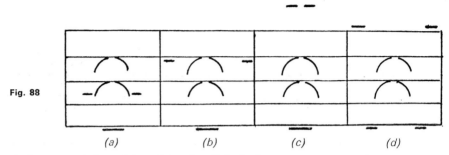

Fig. 88

(a)  (b)  (c)  (d)

(a)  Lying, arms by side of body. (b)  Lying, arms extended to the sides. (c)  Lying, arms above head in line with body. (d)  Lying, feet astride ('star' shape).

Prone lying with legs in more complex positions.

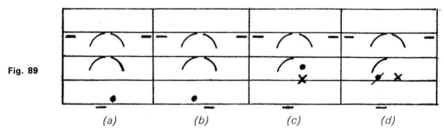

Fig. 89

(a)  (b)  (c)  (d)

(a)  Lying, right leg extended behind, just above the ground.
(b)  As (a) but left foot extended behind.
(c)  Right knee and foot behind. Note that to perform this movement the right hip comes off the ground.
(d)  Similar to (c) but the right foot crosses over behind the body.

## D · **Movements of the Body on the Ground**

### 1. *Rolling*

Rolling is shown by combinations of support signs, supplemented when necessary by direction signs.

The signs for direction of facing apply just the same as when standing erect. If the mover, after standing erect, falls forward on to his face or backward on to his back, he is regarded as retaining the same direction of facing. If he then rolls on to his side, he changes his direction of facing just as he would have done if he had remained upright and rotated his body in the same sense, and exactly the same turning sign is used in all three cases. Suppose he is standing upright facing the right side of the working area: a quarter-turn to the right causes him to face the rear. Now suppose him to have fallen on his back from the original standing position: he rolls on to his right side, once again rotating his body one quarter-turn to the right, and ends facing the rear as before. Then again, suppose him to have fallen on his front from the original position: he rolls on to his left side, once again rotating his body a quarter-turn to the right, and once again ends facing the rear.

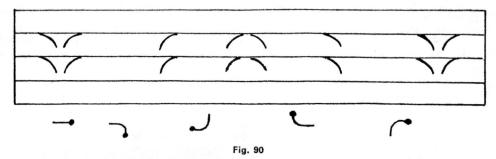

Fig. 90

Start lying supine (on the back). Roll on to the right side, roll on to the front, roll on to left side and return to supine lying.

Note that only the first direction sign is essential: the actions of rolling (and the direction of roll) are indicated clearly by changes in the support signs. In this case, however, the turning signs are used to make doubly clear what is happening.

Forward roll.

Fig. 91

The head and body rounds forward, the roll taking place along the back, finishing in a standing position.

73

Backward roll.

Fig. 92

As above, but the roll is taken from the hips to the shoulders, the legs come over the head and the roll finishes in a standing position.

## 2. Rocking

Rocking of the body while in contact with the ground is shown by taking out the support sign when the relevant part of the body ceases to be supported.

Fig. 93

Start lying prone. Swing arms back bending upper trunk and head backwards and lifting shoulders off the ground. Rock on to the chest, feet lifting behind, hips off the ground. Repeat the action.

Fig. 94

Start lying supine. Swing legs forward, weight comes on to shoulders, swing legs back, weight on to hips (sitting). Repeat the action.

74

## E · A Gymnastic Sequence

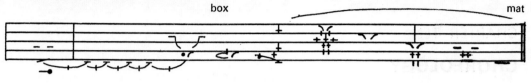

**Fig. 95**

The above example brings together movements on the ground and movements on apparatus.

Run to a box, land on right knee, hands extended to sides, left leg behind. Swing left leg round to side so that it is now in front. Drop on to mat on left foot. Forward roll to standing.

This chapter gives only a brief introduction to the main forms of support. Support on the hands and other body parts is shown by building up from the basic support sign. In the same way, notation can show objects supported or grasped by various parts of the body.

CHAPTER TEN

# CHOREOLOGY

It was in 1947 that Rudolf Benesh came to grips with the problems involved in devising a really practical, precise and efficient system of movement notation. He was impelled to do this because his fiancée Joan Rothwell (a dancer faced with the problems of choreography) told him of the need for such a system, and asked him to invent one.

Being the man he was, Rudolf Benesh never for a moment thought of inventing a system suited only to ballet; in fact he saw at once the need for providing a record of any and every kind of human movement. Fortunately his training as a painter and as a musician provided him with some of the means needed to tackle the difficult problems which faced him, and his flair for science helped him to come to grips with these problems in a scientific way, taking account of new ideas in ergonomics and cybernetics which were coming to the fore at this time (and in fact proved to be vital in the design of a practical movement notation). What was no less vital, he had a highly developed creative gift – something common to the true artist and the true scientist – and so he was able in a remarkably short time to make the intuitive jump which solved problems which had baffled large numbers of very intelligent people for centuries.

This was, of course, only the beginning: as always with major inventions, the detailed development required many years of hard work. During the next seven years he worked intensively on this development in collaboration with Joan Benesh (who became a soloist in what was later called the Royal Ballet, and tested all the developments on a wide variety of ballets in the company's repertoire). It was essential to develop means of showing rhythm and phrasing, dynamics and all other qualities of movement; location, direction of facing and direction of movement; twists, inclinations and displacements of the head and various parts of the trunk; complex positions of hands, fingers, feet, eyes, eyebrows and so on; patterns of movement by groups of varying numbers; support of one person by another; contact with objects; contact with the ground in sitting, lying etc.; and many other things. In all this work of development the Beneshes held fast to certain basic principles which were all-important if the notation was to become a really practical and efficient tool: everything had to be kept simple and visual, with no proliferation of symbols; everything had to be kept consistent, developing logically out of the basic signs; and redundancy had to be kept down to a low level, ensuring the greatest possible economy of time and paper.

By 1955 the notation was complete in all essentials, and was adopted for use in the Royal Ballet and the Royal Ballet School (where it was taught to students); later it was adopted by the Ballet Rambert and by a number of other companies and schools in the United Kingdom and in other countries. This was something quite new in the history of the dance; in fact it brought about a quiet revolution, making possible great economies in rehearsal time, maintaining standards of accuracy in revivals which previously had been impossible, and giving invaluable help to choreographers in their creative work.

Right from the start Rudolf Benesh was concerned with designing and developing the notation in such a way that it would lend itself to a variety of applications, and soon after it was taken into use in ballet it encountered a demand for development as a recording tool in work study. This happened when the notation was included among the major British discoveries in science and technology in the British Pavilion at the Brussels Universal Exposition of 1958; some staff members of the French Centre for Technical Studies of the Clothing Industries saw the display in Brussels and realized that it offered great possibilities in work study. In fact they arranged for Rudolf Benesh to come to the Centre to work on the development of Benesh Movement Notation as a research tool and for use in staff training.

This was the first of many new developments. It gradually became clear that the Notation had great potentialities in many other fields, such as physical education, neurology, physiotherapy, ethnology and copyright: in fact all fields where the precise recording and analysis of human movement-patterns is important. At the same time the work of Rudolf and Joan Benesh and of notators trained by them, preparing choreographic scores of works in the repertoires of the Royal Ballet and other ballet and modern dance companies, began to reveal new aspects of the art of choreography of which even the existence had not been suspected before, because they only became apparent when the work could be studied on paper.

What in fact happened was that a new field of study came into existence – the scientific and aesthetic study through notation of all forms of movement – and this was given the name choreology. At the same time it became clear that a body would be needed to foster and control work in this field, and also to train choreologists – highly skilled specialists able to notate any type of movement. In fact there was a pressing demand for choreologists from dance companies in a number of countries, and it was clear that choreologists would also be needed for advanced teaching and various types of scientific research.

To meet these various needs the Institute of Choreology was established in 1963, and in 1965 this was given a joint grant by the Gulbenkian Foundation, the Pilgrim Trust and the Leverhulme Trust to acquire its own premises and expand its activities in ways which by then were clearly necessary. In June, 1965, its new premises in Barons Court, London, were opened by Jennie Lee, Minister of State with special responsibility for the arts, and ever since then its work has continued to expand as new fields open up.

One of the most important activities of the Institute is the training of choreologists. The students take an intensive full-time course which lasts two years, during which they study all major forms of movement (dance, physical education, remedial work, work study etc.) ; work in notation is integrated with practical studies in each movement field, for experience has shown that any type of movement can only be notated correctly if the person notating it analyses it in complete detail, and to do this he must train his kinaesthetic sense of that style or form by executing it. The students also study art, music, anatomy, kinesiology and the history of dance. Much work is done in composition ; this provides a very good test of the students' understanding of notation, and composition on paper leads to the creation of new forms which before were impossible. Graduates are equipped for many different types of career: company notators, teaching notation at all levels, ethnochoreology (collecting and analysing traditional dances), sociology of dance, work study and scientific research.

In addition to conducting examinations and awarding diplomas to choreologists, the Institute examines and awards diplomas to students who learn notation as an integral part of their professional dance training, and to teachers of notation at various levels of achievement and in various fields of movement. In the early days notation was taught only through the ballet technique, because there was a pressing demand for the teaching of notation to students in ballet schools and also for company notators. Since then other fields have become important, and methods have been developed for teaching notation through them. Experience has shown that notation is best taught at all levels as an integral part of education in a particular type of movement, and this is done in a wide variety of schools, academies, colleges and conservatoires all over the world. (In this respect movement notation is on a par with the alphabet, music notation, and the various symbolic languages of mathematics.) The Institute provides correspondence courses for those who find it most convenient to study in this way.

The establishment of the B.Ed. degree has given special importance to work in movement notation by those concerned with physical education: it is clear that work in any aspect of physical education can only reach academic respectability through the use of notation, and the Institute has set up an Education Department to deal with this aspect of notation. At Chelsea College of Physical Education, Benesh Movement Notation has been taught as part of a research programme in movement notation.

Another very important field for the application of movement notation is medicine. A great pioneer in child neurology and cerebral palsy, Professor Milani (head of the Centro di Educazione Motore in Florence) has found the Benesh Movement Notation is of the greatest value in this field, providing a precise record of normal and abnormal patterns of movement, and a major research project on the development of this use of Benesh Movement Notation is now in hand. In physiotherapy, too, Benesh Movement Notation has proved its value: it is in fact being taught to the student-physiotherapists at the Bürgerspital in Basel.

The Institute keeps in touch with qualified notation-teachers and choreologists all over the world, making sure that work in different fields is coordinated.

One important service provided by the Institute is the maintenance of a movement library, where access is provided to a wide variety of choreographic scores (ballet, modern-dance, Indian classical, historical, national, ethnic etc.) and also to scores in other important branches of movement: gymnastics, games, athletics, remedial work, neurology, work study etc. Copyright in choreograpic works is achieved through registering the scores with the Institute, which is a member of the British Copyright Council.

# CHAPTER ELEVEN

## CONCLUSION

The reader who has worked through the notation examples in Chapters One to Nine will have a clear understanding of the basic principles of Benesh Movement Notation.

If he wishes to carry further his work in Benesh Movement Notation he may like to study with a qualified teacher or lecturer, or take a correspondence course; for information about courses and in fact any aspect of Benesh Movement Notation and choreology, he should get in touch with the Institute of Choreology (4 Margravine Gardens, London, W.6. – Telephone 01–748–7121). Those wishing to undertake advanced studies should enrol for a Choreologists' Course at the Institute.

This book is only an introduction, and does not cover such important aspects of notation as location, direction of movement, patterns of group movement, positions of hands and feet, support, contact with objects, eye movements and other aspects of facial expression, finger movements as used in industry, and so on. Also – and no less important – it does not attempt to teach the equivalent of grammar and spelling in each movement field. All these things can only be learned by studying with a teacher or lecturer or by correspondence courses.

It would be difficult to exaggerate the importance of the invention of Benesh Movement Notation and its adoption within any specific movement field. Like the alphabet, it is precise, simple, economic, fast, universal and objective; like the alphabet (invented in the Middle East nearly 4,000 years ago) it was designed to provide a simple and practical recording tool which *anyone* could use, and because it succeeded in this aim it has increased enormously the possibilities of communication and preservation of movement information. In the past we have expected everyone to become literate and numerate; now the time is coming when we may help them to become choreate as well, opening up a whole new world of precise thinking and imagining for everyone.

A good deal of experience has already been gained in teaching the notation along with other forms of movement over a range of ages from eight onwards. Because of its visuality and simplicity young ballet students find it very easy to master; in fact it helps them understand what they are doing with their bodies, and contributes greatly to the mastery of skills.

In the secondary school the advantages of the notation become very clear. It helps the children to think clearly and logically about movement, strengthens their kinaesthetic sense, and speeds up the development of their awareness of space, weight and time. It is also of great value in composition work: a generalized form of the notation has been developed, and this is used to establish generalized programs which individual children interpret with a wide variety of ideas. The teacher hands out generalized programs (or writes them on the blackboard, or shows them with an overhead projector), and the pupils interpret them in detail, each one of them in his own way. When the ideas are fully developed they can be recorded by teacher or pupil, using the normal detailed notation. It is also possible for children who have been taught the notation to compose directly on paper. It has been found that children greatly enjoy this, and find it exciting and stimulating – some composing movement as freely on paper as others compose in English.

In work in the various branches of physical education at Colleges of Education the use of this notation has many crucial advantages, above all in work for the B.Ed. (which demands a standard of academic respectability and scientific objectivity comparable to that which is normal in other College of Education and University disciplines); and it is just as valuable to lecturers as to students. Those same qualities of simplicity, visuality, precision and so on which adapt it for use by pupils are no less important at College level. Lectures can be planned on paper, in detail, and during the lecture points can be explained clearly and logically; in fact communication between lecturers and students is very much more detailed and effective. As for the students, they can take far more precise and complete notes of everything written and demonstrated – and years later they can read these movement notes as easily as they read their notes of what was said; moreover (as mentioned above) they can use the generalized form of the notation to foster creativity in their pupils by the use of generalized programs. The teacher can use notation to keep a record of the children's creative work and so help them to develop their ideas in a positive and progressive way as they develop from stage to stage. (I shall be dealing with the whole subject of work with generalized programs in a later book.)

Notation is also of great importance at Colleges of Education in making possible the study of movement scores, and the writing of essays and the answering of examination questions with precise movement illustrations, making very clear whether or not the student has fully grasped the points made in the lecture. The stimulus given by notation to disciplined thinking about movement is considerable and important: I know from my experience that there is often a serious dichotomy between what students do in movement (or think they do) and what they actually write down. (Before any movement can be written down, it must be analysed in the mind, using kinaesthetic memory and imagination, and the process of thinking through as far as the written record is a salutory one.) The development of skills is greatly speeded up when understanding is aided by notation: students in fact find that through their study of Benesh Movement Notation they understand many things about movement which before were baffling to them.

Notation is of great value to lecturers in providing them with an infallible test of their success in communicating with students. Sometimes I have worked very hard at explaining a basic principle to students who have not learned notation, and have felt sure that the students understood it, only to find later, on looking at their written work (using the alphabet) that they were unable to apply the principle correctly. Students who had learned Movement Notation handed in work showing a much more assured understanding of the principles.

Generalized programs are just as valuable to stimulating the creativity of students as of pupils; and composition on paper can be developed to a high level, with ideas developing as logically and expressively as in a symphony.

Another important use of notation is in recording the movements of pupils and students; these records can be used for research purposes, and teachers and lecturers can also use notation to exchange ideas by correspondence, as well as reading literature with notation examples and contributing to it themselves. This would greatly assist the building up of the literature on the creative aspect of physical education (i.e. educational gymnastics and dance), in a field which has suffered very much in the past from the sparsity of the available literature.

The possibilities in fields other than education are equally varied. Work in neurology is already well advanced, and with the translation of Benesh Movement Notation into computer languages, many new possibilities are opened up. Ethnochoreology, a new discipline made possible by notation, just beginning to take its place alongside the well-established discipline of ethnomusicology: here there is an exciting field of work for choreologists, since everything they do is bound to be pioneer work. Much the same is true of dance history and criticism: up to now judgements have inevitably been superficial, being based on a fleeting memory of something evanescent moving through time: now, at last, they can be based on the detailed study of scores, and opinions can be backed up by detailed exposition and illustration.

Some hint of the great development we may expect from the extensive use of notation in work in movement may be derived from study of what happened to European music after the perfecting of music notation. Generation after generation of composers continued to enrich traditions of composition, each learning from his predecessor, and there was also a good deal of movement of ideas from country to country: in consequence development was rapid, until the basis was laid for the emergence of geniuses like Bach, Mozart, Beethoven and Verdi, each of whom produced a long series of masterpieces which enriched humanity.

Another field where the development of notation has paid rich dividends is science. The great flowering of science and technology in the last few centuries has to a large extent been made possible by the development of a variety of mathematical notations: computers, for example, could never have been developed to their present efficiency and complexity without the invention of symbolic logic.

With the development of movement notation, corresponding possibilities for creative and scientific development are opened up in all movement fields; much has already happened within the last few years, and I feel sure that we are on the threshold of a variety of exciting new developments.

# APPENDIX

## A · Modern Educational Dance

An extract from the score of *Atomic Goodnight*, staged by Marguerite Causley to music by Charles Koechlin ('Les Bandar-Log') with pupils of Moira House School, Eastbourne. The choreography for other scenes was composed in notation by Marguerite Causley, but for this scene she asked five girls to create their own movements, assigning each of them a strand of the music; the patterns created by the girls were written down afterwards for purposes of research in creativity. The extract shows a series of short solos created by the various girls.

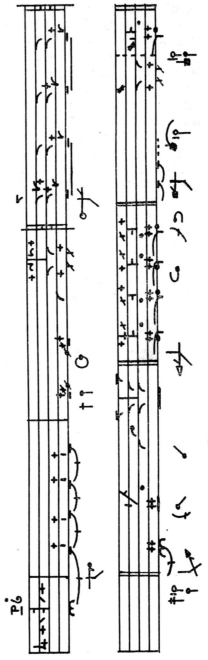

## B · Modern American Dance

A floor sequence.

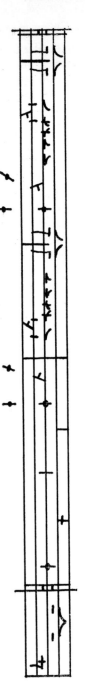

## c · Gymnastics

Educational gymnastics. A sequence of movements worked out and presented as part of final assessment work by Meg Prestidge, student at Chelsea College of Physical Education (autumn 1966).

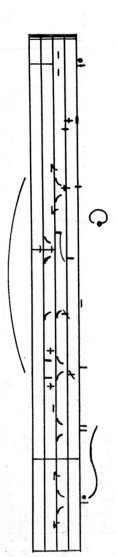

## D · Remedial Exercises

Leg raising in supine position.

## E · Athletics

Hurdling: the approach to the first hurdle, flight over, landing, and run into the second approach.

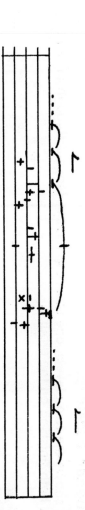

## F · Rugger Tackle

This shows the two players, one throwing himself forward through the air to grasp the other player, both finishing on the ground.

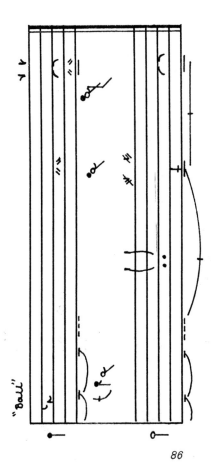

## G · Golf Swing

This illustrates the various sections of the swing; the stance, the swing back, the stroke, the follow through.

## H · Work Study

This shows intricate finger movements whilst using a sewing machine.

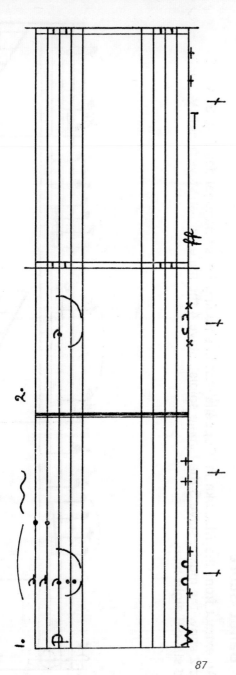

## I · Neurology

Walk of a spastic child.

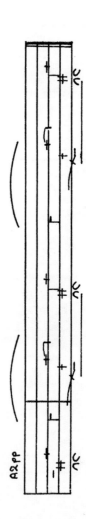

## J · Ballet Score

An extract from the Mazurka in 'Coppélia' Act I., showing Polish national dancing. Staves 1 and 2 show the music, stave 3 the female soloist, stave 4 the male soloist, stave 5 eight women and stave 6 eight men.

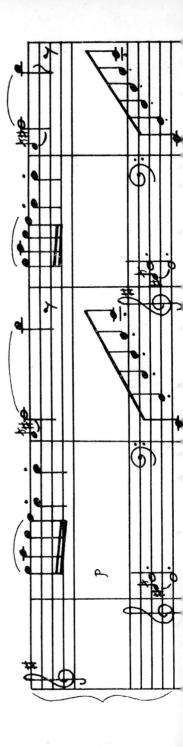

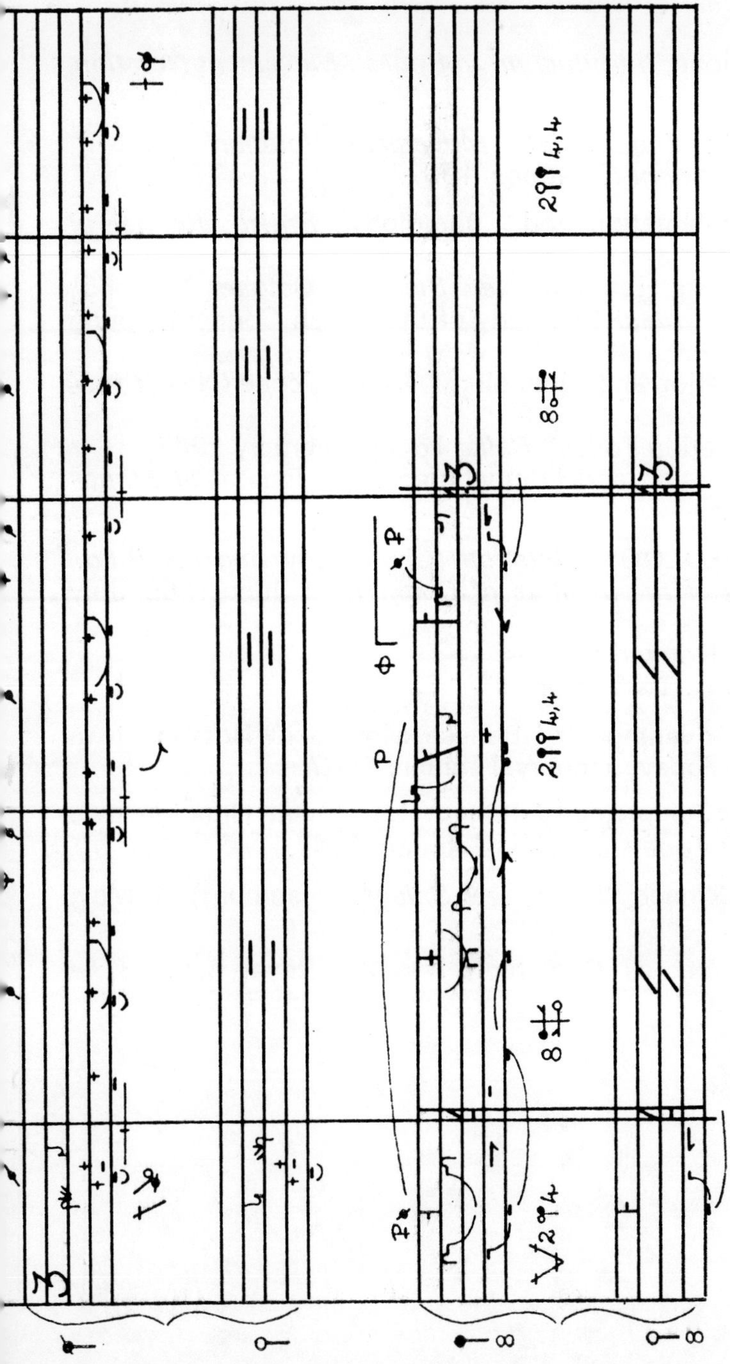

# BIBLIOGRAPHY

1. BENESH, Rudolf and Joan, *Introduction to Benesh Movement Notation*, London, 1955.

2. CURL, Gordon F., *'An Enquiry into Movement Notation'* (Part I), *Laban and Benesh Movement Notations*, 1967.

3. HALL, Fernau, 'Dance Notation and Choreology', *British Journal of Aesthetics*, January 1964.
   'An Alphabet of Movement Notation', *New Scientist*, October 28, 1965; republished in *Music in Britain* (quarterly of the British Council), spring 1966.
   'Benesh Movement Notation and Choreology', *Dance Scope* (New York), Fall 1966.
   'Benesh Movement Notation Today', *Ballet Today*, February 1967.
   'Benesh Movement Notation and Ethnochoreology', *Journal of Ethnomusicology*, May 1967.

4. INSTITUTE OF CHOREOLOGY, *Notation, Choreology and the B.Ed.*, 1966; *Progress reports of the Institute of Choreology*, June 1965, July 1966, December 1966.
   Progressive Readers of Notated Studies.
   *Dances from the Classics* (Two volumes).

5. MORRICE, Norman, 'Advantages of Benesh Movement Notation to a Choreographer', *Ballet Today*, January–February 1967.

6. MOSSFORD, Lorna, 'Advantages of Benesh Movement Notation to a Ballet Company', *Ballet Today*, January–February 1967.

7. 'Choregraphie: Fussball nach Noten', *Der Spiegel* (Hamburg), 1 May, 1967.

8. WORTH, Faith, 'My Work as Choreologist to the Royal Ballet', *The Dancing Times*, June 1967.

Marguerite Causley is a lecturer at Chelsea College of Physical Education, Eastbourne.

She brings to her work in physical education and notation a wide background of teaching experience in mathematics, science, art and various specialized movement fields (notably gymnastics, modern and national dance and swimming). After deciding to specialize in movement education she did further study at Chelsea College of Physical Education, and went on to teach modern educational dance at secondary level, as well as doing choreography in various styles, and studying American modern dance.

Her study of Benesh Movement Notation with Rudolf and Joan Benesh made her realize the importance of this system in modern educational dance and in fact in all branches of physical education. She was the first to receive a teacher's notation diploma in educational movement from the Institute of Choreology, and has done pioneer work teaching Benesh Movement Notation at Chelsea College of Physical Education as part of a research project organised by Gordon F. Curl. She has done pioneer work in choreography composed in detail on paper, with notation.

She is at present engaged in research in the use of notation, in the analysis and development of creativity in various forms of movement education, and in the development of logical, progressive syllabi and programs for modern educational dance.

# NOTES